BURN ALL NIGHT

BURN ALL NIGHT

NEW AND SELECTED POEMS

ELIZABETH ELLIOTT

ATHENA BOOKS
GOLDEN HILL PRESS
SPENCERTOWN, NEW YORK

First Edition, March 31, 1998
© Elizabeth Elliott, 1997.

This book is printed on acid-free paper.

Library of Congress Cataloging-in-Publication Data

Elliott, Elizabeth, 1932-
    Burn all night : new and selected poems / Elizabeth Elliott. -- 1st ed.
        p.   cm.
    ISBN 1-889029-02-5 (alk. paper). -- ISBN 1-889029-04-1
(alk. paper)
    I. Title.
PS3555.L577B87   1998   811'.54--dc21   97-48285 CIP

This book was set in Adobe Caslon
    by Kath Moran of North Wing Studios, Stuart, Florida

Published in the United States of America by
    Athena Books, an Imprint of Golden Hill Press, Inc.,
    Spencertown, New York 12165

Acknowledgement: The poem "So Long a Shade" was originally published under the title "Helios," in *The Partisan Review,* 1979.

For Clint

Table of Contents

ONE

TWO

❖

BURN ALL NIGHT

ONE

Burn All Night

The fiery soul of that fire
Glows at last,
The wet wood was hard to start,
Unlike the terrifying timber of the fall;
      We rake the outer edges in toward the flame,
      But stay behind it,
      For the heat of its advance,
      Before the January wind,
      Is brutal;
It took a long time to get this pile,

      A long time to get it burning,
      Now it will burn all night.

Resist Me Death!

Death is no stranger but a favored guest
whose ways are still unknown, and yet
The darkness into which I float to rest
Is kinder than the hearts with which I've grown.

Death is no stranger, and yet
Death! Stranger to the thought
than hands to fish,
less welcome than a lure you can't resist,

resist me now!
Turn back!
Your way is north
and mine is south.

I work toward apple brine,
break of serried hedge,
water pausing, and the scrolls of leaf.

I'm going south,
to peace and the song of birds
to a love I had thought would never call—
—Death!

No, not me,
not now!
Be content with having the power to make me flee,
content with being the dark I fear,

content with any role you choose
save that of being my deliverer!

Pared

The moon is hot in a hot sky
pared smaller each night
as crickets jaw in their stiff fields

Pared smaller each night
as insects shave
and nothing yields

As insects insist their stubbled note
and no thing yields
Cut is the moon's bright glass

Nothing shields
Cut is the bright glass
jawed to a limp shard

Cut is the moon's light caught
its mirror pared to a bluejay's tongue
Dried insects are eating the moon

Have eaten the moon
and the sky hangs high in a groaning heat
great darkness pregnant with dread not rain

Dread not rain—

Spring:
Between Two Soggy Glooms

A new low is close on the heels of the low that has just departed,
but today,
    into the riff and quiver of not-yet-summer sun,
    into the ground shadowed by hawk,
    into the stillness
    quilting the acres his eyes possess,
pierce ninety-nine uncontrollable twitters of loosed birds;
    when the hawk dips on up and over,
    is gone to the county next,
    when the passage of his dark is done,
each leaf shakes to the swing of an on-again-off-again breeze,
a hip-jointed, jitter-bug this-a-way-that,
    each branch tremors
    with ninety-eight uncontrollable
    and with a hundred and ninety-eight controllable,
throats tuned to their strummed skill,
tuned to the shook frets of green-sprung trees,
tuned to the absence of hawk in a cloud-blooming sky,
    until
perfume of cadence silvers the air,
sunnysides rapture,
silvers across to

the blue evermore river widening in pace with the steady miles
                    of walking mountains.

How Rose Can A Rose

How rose can a rose
        become?
Is daily perfection
not yet its limit

but more, tomorrow,
and yet tomorrow?

And are we,
like the rose becoming rose
        constrained from being also
        a perfect tree?

        If it was the rose
        that we were born to be?

        If it was the rose.
        Ah—

So Long A Shade

I am Helios,
I go everywhere and am forever fixed,
The light I shed I cannot comprehend,
For I see however brilliant is that light,
Deeper the attendant shade;
  I am of two minds,
  Sometimes I see my light and know it,
  Sometimes I see only shade and know this;
The warmth I give consumes me,
And my laughter is a handful of flowers
Torn from a bush of thorns,
My tears the song of sorrow
For the man of Being, who cannot simply Be;
  What light is this that casts so long a shade?

Angels Going By

Angels pass
and the air is lighter

for them
the air is dense with trails
and their eyes already
have sent messages they come

streaming with light
traffic of the universe

Harry says
there are more than ever

and thinks
it's time to count them out
by watt
or slanting weight
not simply as before.

after a lapse
language is the denser game

quiet there
in the marbled columns

the one
expects the two to crowd
but it's late
to think of flight

fire and ice
rain and the peaceful wind

False Eye and True

A thinprick stab is the False I,
(Sometimes to be translated False Eye, never False One),
A needle-ever going rusty, jabbing furious and weak
Into the stony hide of Sere Elephant;
It cannot move Seer Elephant, it cannot impede his progress,
But people seeing done such viciousness,
This last-hope action of False I,
Wonder if just this once Sere Elephant won't be diverted.
And thus wondering, the people get distracted.

But ah! Let us hasten, love, through this silver dawn, this
                                      green green day,
Lightstruck by water-rise from the great magnetic fall,
Through this air wove thin of waternets thrown sparkling
                            upon the sun and barely dry,
Let us hasten with happiness held in our magic-holding hands,
                            and see how the

True I, a rug of heavy silk,
Is flung with perfect timing,
With perfect swirling balance,
Up upon the broad-gait back of Seer Elephant;
How evenly, how smoothly, it falls and lies,
How rich its colors ascend these dawning skies;
Tapestried silk, oh field of verde-blue,
Cracking the eye with sharpness, with holy hope of blue,

Blue that plunging all too deep can yet not stay but
Rising swiftly,
Staggers Heaven, who is cobalt-lazy.

Blue silk woven with fields of flowers,
Blue silk marbling the mountain towers
Blue silk, blue silk, dizzy my days,
Blue silk show me the thousand ways, sing me the thousand
songs,
Your golden tassel-tears of praise cry out upon my heart and
say,
"How you have heaped me with beauty and with very joy,
How may my voice be loud to call thy name,
Sowing seeds of thy praise with a broadfling love of my wide
heart,"
Oh heavy, heavy rug, bespeaking care,
Bespeaking care in all things, and bearing no name, no name
but thine.

It is such blue that True I is on the back of Sere Elephant;
And neither does the heavy silken rug impede the progress
Of Sere Elephant, but rather crowns him with ceremonial love,
Enhancing his great dignity,
And delighting the eyes of his subjects.

13

Keep Me As The Apple Of Thy Eye;
Hide Me In The Shadow Of Thy Wings

I
Attach permanently
to instrument. Serial no. 24346 035

This cover
is provided with an interlock
for protection against shock.

For servicing
always remove cover completely.

II
At the center lies the pool; surfacing, they laugh,
blow water, shake their heads, stroke once,
and dive again. The long dry heat is gone,
and water falls extravagantly away,
it asks no proof, it falls playfully
away, it is completely there, it gives
no directions, it falls exuberantly away,
it falls directly into its own self.

Before the long day, a long swim.
After the long day, a swim feels good.
Out of the play and the pool they climb,
And beneath the skimpy towels their faces set.

III
Put off your shoes from your feet
for the place where you stand is holy.

The management shall not be responsible
for the loss of money, jewels,
and valuable packages.

In case of loss by fire,
or overwhelming force—

IV
At the center lies the pool.
On three sides, two banks of chairs
face the pool, on two corners
stand folded umbrellas.

On three sides, behind
the chairs lie three strips of grass,
crabgrass, dully green and sharp.
At the center lies the pool.

Behind the chairs and grass
stand three glass walls, behind the walls
the double rooms with outlets.
At the center lies the pool.

"Do you remember Paris? The first walk
we took in the Tuilleries? The white
            sand, the fountains,
            the children and the trees?"
"I remember." On the fourth side
are the cars, lined up neatly
            on the pitted asphalt
            of the parking lot for cars.

On the fourth side are the cars.
"After our drinks let's take a stroll
            in the park. It will be cool.
            It will still be light."

"Do you remember the first time we saw
Monet's waterlilies in the Orangerie?"
            "Yes, I remember." From the rooms,
            from the grass, from the banks of chairs,

        ("There is a view."
        "There is always a view."
        "No, I mean this view is beautiful.
        It is beautiful to be there.
        Come with me. It will do you good.")
At the center lies the pool and when
there are people in the pool,
            or sitting in the chairs,
            or crossing the stiff grass,

or when they sit in their double room
looking out, over the grass, the chairs,
        the pool, they see the cars.
        They see the parking lot and cars.

V
Thou dost lay them in the dust of death,
yet at the scent of water they will bud.
At the center lies the pool.
There are people
        waiting in the double rooms,
        crossing over on the sharp grass,
        resting and watching from the chairs,
        diving and surfacing
        and laughing in the pool,

There are people
        who will go to the cars
        will unlock them
        and drive them away.

        In the memory of these people
        lie things not told here.

Kindly notify the office
if their departure will be delayed.

Sources
Title: Psalm 17:8
Lines 62 and 63: Joshua 5:15
Lines 81 and 82: Psalm 22:15 and Job 14:9

17

Rodeo

Rider to go quietly into herd,
    cut out animal
    run him down
    rope him
Healer to come in and heal animal,
    leave dally on the horn
    get off horse
    take rope
Rider to go down and touch animal,
Rider to go quietly into herd,
To go quietly to herd,
To pasture, to go quietly to pasture,
To the fields of flowers raised for seed,
Rider to go quietly to pasture,
To be raised for the purpose of seed,
To be raised, to be raised for the animal,
For the healing of the animal,
For the healing and the going to seed,
    For the healing,
    For the purpose
    For the going to seed.

TWO

Abrupt the Rose

To the bud
A rose
Must sound like thunder.

Soft drumming hint
        Then rich explosion,
As peal upon peal of sulky rumble
And petal upon petal
        Springing the rose to bloom
Furnish flower to the night.

The Body's Joy

Poem for Anne Sexton because of her poem:
"Little Girl, My String Bean, My Lovely Woman"

Lucky the girl whose mother sees womanhood
begin to bloom upon her daughter
and can accept and love that this be so;

Lucky the girl whose mother does not see
this fruitfulness of summer on its way
and out of envy burn the crop
with remarks that wither, deprecate,
or fill with fear;

Lucky the girl who can lie in fever,
trusting her face into the hand of she
who gave her birth, and while she sleeps
her mother dreams for her,
the pleasures of her body,
beginning to come near;

These pleasures, so acute they take the form
of lemons that become a map of all the world,
and this becomes the way her body,
when she's born a second time,
will know geographies of love;

Geographies of continental drift,
of hands and eyes and cunt and skin,
geographies of sweat and swamp and lakes at morning
when the mutual greeting of a smile
is all the world has need of to insure
its long, primordial spin;
For all is swelling here;
behind the heat of fever in her face
the garlic buds engorge,
and nearby apples begin their swell,
though true, till now,
she's been more like the promise of a bean;

Lucky the girl whose mother does not take alarm,
but says to her daughter,
Darling, let your body tie you in, in comfort,
and know there is nothing in your body
that will ever tell you lies,
that all this which seems new
is telling you its truth;

Lucky the girl whose mother,
like a wise old tree,
can reassure her stringbean girl;
Lucky the girl whose mother loves to make way
for the season of her daughter's time.

Double Play

When she's in the kitchen
her man gets a run.
Twice he does.

And because it counts,
she decides
she'll stay there when he's at bat.

Her husband,
shouting out
encouragement,

tells her what is going on.
She longs to see,
but is convinced

her absence from the screen
will bring the team
good luck.

It does.
Hitting in the fat
of the bat, it wins.

At dinner,
her husband tells her
he had heard the score

at breakfast,
that tonight's game
was just a rerun,

that he had known, all day,
her team would win.
A rerun then.

They could see it Saturday again,
perhaps next month,
in the wrap-up of the season's games.

It will go in a can
and be taken out sometimes.
But gradually,

over the years,
people will begin to see
a shadow on their screens.

And Zenith and Sony and GE
will not be able
to shake it loose,

nor make the image clear;
no matter
how many circuit cells

are shuffled
in the magnate case,
the shadow stays.

It darkens with the passing
of each year.
It is the shadow

of my little birdlike
mother running
into the kitchen

and staying there
so her team
will get the luck.

Welcome

When I was sick and lay abed,
I had two fellows at my head,
Two beside me where I lay,
Two on top throughout the day,
Two beneath me, two below
If there were more I could not know;
And in the dream I had that night,
A space I saw, so sweet, so light,
But just the shape and size of me,
And all within, where none could see;
I knew this space had once been dead,
But now it moved, on life it fed,
And even as I watched, it grew,
Pulsed outward, like a heart that knew
A welcome lay beyond the bounds
Of past conditions, early wounds,
With smiling ease, it moved and passed,
Broke through the skins of flesh, at last
Its being mingled with my own,
And some shy grace I had not known
Caressed my room and all its things,
My looking glass, my comb, my rings;
Each pair of fellows then arose,
And stood within this glowing air,
They each were me and we were there
And I was them, if this be so
God only knows.

A Very Brief Affair

Poem for Monday Number One

Step out with a stranger and he falls into my bed,
Just a saunter to the nearest pub,
And with nothing on, he's here, at dawn, instead.

The city passes angles on its hat,
The messages escape by tube.
A tower leans a little to the left,
And no one tells you you are crude.

But daisies in the morning milk, now surely
It has gone a little far,
But then, his eyes are velvet and his mouth like open silk.

Poem for Monday Number Two

He's got a wife he's not about to leave,
Although they've lived apart for years,
And too, he's had a mistress
Who, although she sounds neurotic as a crab in pants,
Has swayed upon his life for long,
The way a bramble sways
And grasps the maple trunk;
Between the two there isn't room for me.
He thinks so, but I don't.

Poem for Monday Number Three

The groin goes fishing in the lakes of fire,
Narrow and shaded by high cliffs;
The soul and the intelligence
Set off for wide, clear lakes
Where mountains kiss their own image.

But no fish are found in either place.
All the fish are being caught
By a man who doesn't speak,
Or, when he does, you have to lean to hear.

He's been fishing now for years,
Pulling in his lines,
Supplying the markets without trouble.

The postcards of the fiery lake,
The postcards of the mountain lake,
Are sold to tourists who pass through.

Superiority of A Fly

To contemplate
the tastebuds
on the feet of flies,

    the fluctuating
    input
    to the gut

is to learn to shake our heads with awe,
for what the fly requires, it has.
We two live,
though I require you
yet have you not,

    though you have me
    and yet
    require me not.

And so, this fly, who cannot read
the tallest print and does not care

what age a rock,
he is,
it seems

    perfected,
    quite
    finished

in detail, where we are rude
unsynchronized, and halt.

Yet you and I,
two doors
and three

> long distances
> apart,
> prefer

our damaged flight and try to keep
this Perfect Being off our food.

Love Grew On Us

Love grew on us
as common grass
    fell on us
      as common rain,
Love laid on us
a common kiss
      as we held hands,
      then kissed again.

Love ran in us
as windblown fire,
      love swarmed in us
      and stung as bees,
Love flowed in us
as water pure,
      though speechless now,
      we walked the seas.

Love drew us on
as moons are drawn,
    lured us on
      as night drew nigh,
Love pressed us on
for we would drown
      in one another's
      fiery sigh.

Love wounds in us
as love doth well,
   love wraps us in
   her mending wings,
Love seals in us
her common death,
   from which the lifting
   phoenix sings.

Glasses

Your glasses are all right,
Not if we're like *this;*
OK, they're in my hand,
Feel them? No. Here, silly,
I'm polishing them on your back so they can see,
Oiling the little hinges
So their arms can reach
And clasp your head.

Their eyes will look into yours,
Be kissed asleep by your lashes,
And gummed by lying in bed.

Oh dear, my hat was there too.

If He Is Gone

If I may not have him in my bed,
    Then just across the room,
And if not that, then down the hall,
    Our windows open on the same tall bloom;

And if I may not have him in my house,
    Then down the road will have to do,
Around the corner, in the village,
    Or out into the country, perhaps a mile or two.

But if he may not be as near as this,
    My heart will still be song,
To know that he is homeward bound,
    To even know that he is far, and will be long;

And if I knew that he would never come again,
    But for another knew the lover's anguished ache,
I still could smile, knowing him to be,
    But if he is nowhere now, if he is gone,

    —my heart will break.

For My Daughter, Suddenly Become A Bride

What is this miracle of my firstborn,
      a merest wicket then,
      resting on my arm,
      a fragrant nuzzle grown to cry and scamper,
      grown to talking child, a rouser to rabble,
who used the proffered hand to jump the whole flight;
Who is this bright instigator,
      and my morning's star?

      Oh treasure!
      Oh meddler!
      who came with laughter in every size,
even in very narrow widths,
      even with platform heels,
      and always with open toes,
no strings attached and no return address,
gift-wrapped and ready for the dance.

      Oh first love,
      struck like a flinder from my own young years,
How did she make a trapeze of time and fly away?
How did she trespass away from me
      and into her own farm-fiddling,
      how did she trespass into her own castle,
      into her own four-lane kitchen of singing jets,
and rice-creamed blueberries, ivory and blue and gold?

How did you not leave and yet, now, be going?
What is this outrage, this trick called Time,
    a fastidious driver to old age,
    no union can change the wage this Boss pays,
    or in any way protest, call "Halt!" or run away.
This Time that gives and takes, then turns
and gives again what it must take again
    all in the too-quick reflex of one old wrist.

Dear Ib, be off, dance in the circle of Time and Love
in the surge and ripple of briar and burn,
    in your story's beginning
    your story's return,
    And I, unchanged, rooted,
    buried to the very quick in love,
    asks not a moment back,
but urge you on, but urge you on.

Small Forks in the Wrong Drawer

A twinge, a somersault of love, to see
    the small forks in the wrong drawer;
    they mean: my daughter was just here;

Instantly the morning aches are gone,
    I am back in yesterday when she left on the first train,
    back in the day before, when she arrived,
I think how I watch her soul paint beauty on her face;

    A bluebird feeds on the rail,
    the first I've ever seen,
    But oh, the small forks in the wrong drawer.

THREE

Blame Me!

Blame me! I did it all, the S and L's,
    the gore of ripping arms from shoulders,
    the snuff films and the rapes in parks,
I did this all, so come make justice here;
    Leave the courtrooms and the pressrooms
    of the crazed sad cities and find me, your culprit
    in the top of the beech,
in the root of the birch,
    on the thumb of the old gray owl;
    I'm wicked as sunlight in a milkglass cup,
wicked as crickets pinching songs in the rain,
    wicked as shells washed ashore in the storm,
    wicked as dawn on the eyes of love.
Here are my wrists
    limp with moondust,
    place manacles there and I'll come;
Here is my leg,
    slap a chain there,
    I'll clank myself over to your prison cells;
Here is my head,
    place your noose there;
    let me swing in the lovely lusts of May.

When In Doubt Hold On To Your Animal

I fell down a cistern the right way
and there was a long story crawling up/it
didn't know it would come out
and I didn't want to say it was
over-involved with itself as it was
but I felt sorry for an animal/
that had been dragged in as someone's pet
and then forgot after I'd passed it a few
times I asked if a change of scene
would please/the animal promptly
took me at my hand and we became nice
and acquainted in the darkness going down
by that I only mean we were still
together at the bottom when the door
of this long fall/opened onto a scene
where it would be good to have my animal
and where it sure needed me a yokel
out of the past I was and no one
birthed me till I realized/I hadn't breathed yet
and in a fury of slightly meditated action
I birthed myself only to find/the hands
that caught me were the same as held
me in and when I'd got into my shoes I took off
really keen/and terrified well
that tells/you how I happened to get
here, no, right here, now,

it's OK you know, I did the same thing myself,
it doesn't mean we have to chop
our hands off at the wrists.

hey, take it easy.

What Provides

In repressed explosion of distress,
There came fatigue to haunt the will.
    The lust to grow
        Grown stained
    The need to heal
        Held back
    The hope to find
        Found soured
    The need to bind
        All bound in black,
All bound in black, and the careful search,
For the word that is just,
    Gives way to a cry
        Crooned low,
    Sheers back to the time,
        Now shorn of seed,
When a child in the flowering of the field,
    Ignored what provides, aborted the yield.

Big Browns

Occasionally I do a favor for a East European cop,

> Randy, back out! The wall's poured,
> not block!

Lean along a custom line, along the soft spots
of the need I know of. Pig-perfect I—

> Randy's my brother with rickety
> tavi-tunes that puddle the dry
> banks, lace milk with scotch.

I winch a john, place a placket
of the stuff to where it won't be reached.

> The boon-dock he'd like to land is suicide,
> heave round toward a cleat, his own.

They trust me, they're right, why would I lie
they're my pension plan, my IRA, Club Med,

> Lucky Randy's loony.
> He'd be a danger to a full deck.

I wonder if he'd make it through the block.

Black Wind And A Dog

Flipping the whole sleek page,
flipping it fast over and above and across the county
      lines,
dismantling the gossip of hen and pol,
shuffling the round white eggs of the altered, the
      sports, the loners and spooks,
dismaying the racket of clubs met over booze—
the black wind prowls from the north.

The black wind, its black ears so deep they hear the
      ocean two hundred miles away,
the black wind, its tongue so wide it licks the green up
      out of the corn,
a tail to knock nesting stars out of the thrash of
      the trees,
paws shod to pad the smoke of the stacks, the smoke in
      the talk over high wires,
eyes glared to a distance two miles high and two states
      south,
and silver hung from belly fur.

With teeth like farm equipment, the black wind bites
      down.
It bites up and it shreds hens ears corn forks stars
      clubs eggs and comfortable politicians.
It roams at will and Will moves indoors,
it drives Harry and Sandra and Bucky off the bridge
      bulging from pole to pole,
into the river singing and the dog makes it to shore.

The dog makes it to shore. And then what?
It's a miserable thing to see a dog stand like that,
filthy wet, curled fur slick against its bones,
it's a miserable thing, that dog, alone down there,
everyone behind shut doors watching a blue eye,
not a friendly watch open for simple help.

Bilious Barbara

Bilious Barbara grew a beard
and splashed her gold till people stared,
she didn't ask before she bitched,
she didn't know that she was feared,
or how the children howled and ran,
she only saw the botch her gold seemed

to make of it

as though no matter how I try
something is against me,
oh I have a very fine therapist,
I really feel very good about myself.

Almost Prayer

This is the last time I'll escape
north
the last time I'll weasel out of facing what I owe.

This is the last escape
out of the bottom
of a well, cooled and deep with tears.

This is the frogged princess.

Time Present

This is the garden,
clay when we moved in,
      some said it could be potter's clay
      if that's what we meant to do,
but we both had memories
of a garden,
      so we brought in manure,
      straw and manure—until at last—
      most things grow.

What? You say you know this?
      You don't mean to press me?
      But you are. You are pressing me,
      you forget that I'm old.
I repeat the things that mean a lot.
      Let me be. Look—

The heat has done the spinach in;
      funny how things thrive
      in a certain place
      and never bloom in others.
Do you remember how privet
grew in Amagansett yet here
      it barely lives?

Stop! Stop telling
me that! Take your hand
off my arm! It isn't true!
        Look, it's a lovely day.

        The eggplants will be large this year.
        The only thing the rabbits leave alone.
                Parmesan cheese.
                I must get some more from Murray's.
        Better marbled than the stuff up here.
Let me go! Stop telling
me that take your hand, no
        I'll stay here. Go
        home
I'll weed until my husband comes.
                Down there! My husband
                is down there. What
        did you say? What? Tell me!
        Look at me, what did you
                tell me then?

        No! My children! No!
And where else? Oh, but no,
say no truth, isn't, isn't, oh
        no, say it isn't true.

                    •

        Leave me now. I'll stay here.
        Leave me here with them,
        with this, this perfect world
        I'll put my chair
                under the cherry tree.

51

The animals will go blind.
    You didn't know?
    Why not. You didn't know. Nor I.
And the birds blind as well.
    The birds will fly in panic,
    fly up through the thickets and woods,
and in panic break their wings.

        Oh world!
        Think of the panic
        and the roaring.
    And it is done?

You say it's done?

        •

No one is innocent of this.

        Leave me.
        Go in yourself.
Of course get the neighbors.
I know my cellar's good.
No, I can't.
        I'll not go in again.
How could I look at things?

Ingredients so complex to make life.
The albums of two marriages.
        The furniture that I store
        until my children have houses
        of their own.
The ironing left over from last fall.

Oh speechless bleeding

A thousand details feed this fountain.
An extraordinary thing
that no one will ignore.
        No delicate and expensive ship sail on.
        No Daedelus undo this maze

The E flat fugue I practice.
                Oh world! What wound!
                No music.

I won't
        be able to bear this long.

                    •

                Bring me a bowl.
                I'll french the beans
                out here. And let it fall
on me, as it falls on the buttercup leaves,
as it falls on the green and the weed-rimmed pond.

They say the sky turns brown.
                A sepia wash perhaps.
                Goya should be alive.
                I will let it fall on me,
        and cry out as the chickadee goes blind,
                small feathered fist
                faltering toward a perch
        to crash the tree,
        to miss the tree,
                and rake a poisoned sky.

All poisoned. Nothing
uncontaminate. The only living
    buried underground.

    The garden is so quiet.
    Watered well. The tomatoes staked.

      soft silo of my
    mouth, the panic rises in my

      blood, the atoms

fly. I am not

        holding together, frenching

the beans and putting

      my feet

    in the

          warm loam.

Consume It To An Ash

The satisfactory thing in watching flame,
      its cardinal breast,
      its leap of wings,

is the unreluctant sense it always brings
      of certain satisfaction
      of its aim;

it knows that it consumes the chosen wood,
      and will consume it
      to an ash;

I'd consider it quite brave,
      but rash, if wood held private
      hopes, misunderstood.

lament and curse

holy all these, our victims
—of wormwood, drought and ring of fire—
holy their cries of shock,
holy their fear and the loosening of the bowels
                      in fear,
holy their dread,
and their convictions melted down in doubt,

holy the process of their good bones breaking,
their good flesh prodded, poisoned, drowned,
their beautiful eyes engraved with images that
drive into their minds and make them mad,

holy their sorrow that lasts as long as shadows
run before the sun,
holy their slight recoveries, a smile returned,
a moment free of strain,
holy the therapists who reach out,
    teach them to dare to move
    who can bear to hear the black dreams,
    the sudden hate they hate,

holy the old one who uses what he has to bring
them help,
holy those hearts that see and hear and read these things
    and pity,
    and feel afraid themselves,
    and curse that they have not the power to help,
    have not the knowledge to prevent,

56

holy all those who suffer in this unholy time,
    all those who suffer for the ones in pain,
unholy the ones who set all suffering aside,

evil the ones who have the power
    and do not use it for relief,
condemned the ones who use a single person's
    suffering for gain.

Where Do I Go?

Why do my friends die?
Where do I go when they all die?
Go where they go?
To the slit in the tree where the moon comes up?
To the break in the wall where the cop-car rolls?
To the vein in the leaf where the grannybird dined?

      Oh the moon comes up,
      the wagon rolls,
      the grannybird dines on nets and holes.

      Nets and holes and dines on mirth,
      on cocained wine and sullen birth;
      Oh suffer such pangs in the morning!

      Give a wide berth to my mate now,
      And I'll give one to ye now,
      But shoot me a bad one and I'll be gone by morning.

Why were my friends born?
Why was I born, to be their friend throughout?
At the top of the hill where the cherry grows?
At the mouth of the stream my dead friend knows?
In starlight hiding the heart of the rose?

FOUR

Under The Sword of Damocles

Terrible children, spawned in a dark we
              thought to leave,
Mouthing filth in our own basements,
Abasing themselves to our command, to
              our suggestion,
Sniggering and gagging toward their full
              size.

Manacled among cheese spreads and their games,
Our men, our women, run away.

The One You Meant To Save

Oh I beg you to beware
Of what you go to kill;
In your justified and inexcusable rage
You may find a great giant
Crashed about your feet,
Great thorny, leafy, head,
Sticky with interrupted life,
Asprawl across the doorway to your home,
Great arms asplintered in your path,
Enormous trunk
Crushed across the one you meant to save,
Trembling roots between you and the sky.

Even the Most Wounded

Even the most wounded of sore spaces,
even the driest, most spiked, abandoned,
even the dumps where nothing further is dumped,
behind the last of the lots deserted by the fathers,
even here grows the wild phlox.

if you can be happy

there is less nonsense than there used to be,
more right to get out with your own clues;
I'd turn it over to you
but I find I've changed and would rather go on.

A Place In Time

All things take their place in time
which opens for them
as a woman opens her jacket on coming into a room,
and when it has come to be,
and every person has been taxed,
and every person seated in the seat to which he can
        always return,
and every person heard by at least one of his own exact
        kind,
when all this, and all other events,
that were to take place, that could have taken place,
        in the room,
when all this is just now done,
we easily see, through a door we had not seen before,
an other room, to which it is time now, to go,
and we leave with no regrets,
not looking back because we know we have forgotten
        nothing,
and we know if it is not a seat we will be given,
        the seat to which we can always return,
and we know if we are not taxed and not heard, as we
        have always been and needed to be, taxed and
        heard,
it does not matter, we know it will be whatever it is,
as full and correct as we who go there
now are also full and correct.

Grief Repetitious and Unassuaged

Beautiful sufficient river,
A dead raccoon in the third lane of the six.

How far had he come?
Was this the third?
Or perhaps he'd climbed the divider
and this was the fourth?

How far he had come!
But oh why?
When the woods were there?

Invasion

In the striped shade below the deck,
the vines survived both darkness
and the patient probing of the blade.

Like living scum they hugged the beams,
drifted, hunched in insect bitten waves of leaf,
over the deck's edge; they loll now among the chairs;

they are crawling their low profiles toward the house.
They see the slack shingles,
the wasps that bore an access to the rooms,

they eye the door that's tilted off its frame,
the soffits where the phoebe nests,
and the window it takes too long to close.

One goldenrod disdained to creep the floor,
but stands two feet above a central crack,
I lean to pull and hear the creaking in the deck.

On the level I prefer to live
I applaud this search and thrust,
I sentimentalize the green that requires no spade or
pot.

On the level where I fear,
I know I have one winter more.

Not In Spite

In spite of the new green,
in spite of the Easter Mass of Birds,

in spite of the long light laying blessed hands
      against the swelling of the day,
in spite of all that ripples out and ties the apron
      of the world with floured hands,

the rain is damp,
we need a fire against the cold.

Patterns in the Blood and Stars

The harbors of heaven are full,
Luxurious with stars,
No turbulence disturbs safe anchorage;
Beyond, who knows what skies of storm
Still churn the outer barriers of reef,
What outer swell of unknown sea?

Light rows to us from distances so far
A thousand years is but one fading stroke;
On the fingers of my stiffening hand
I count four such human strokes
And catch the dreadful distance still to go.
The evening news has left a sorrow in my head.

The dog trots up the hill;
Orion's six stand tilted
In the channel of the driveway trees;
The chilling night turns blue,
Tuned in to cold that burns the eye;
But so adjusted. Nothing I need fix.

I sleep; earth turns; it seems Orion's six
have tacked against the summit of the sky,
Caught a solar breeze, sailed down, and now,
One telltale's breath from dawn,
Still in formation but deep in the west,
Stand tilted on the frosty window-pane.

Oh harmless constellation! Not stars,
but acts create our earthly constellations:
The formation of those in Arrogance who "know,"
Are certain they are "right" or "best," and
therefore can exclude, deport
or kill what secretly they fear;

The formation of Never Have Enough
of always needing the crutch of power;
The formation of Control Through Fear.
Such constellations our minds of heaven know well.
Who would not rather brave space's outer seas
Than shelter in a harbor with such sharks?

If a thousand years is but a fading stroke,
How long, how terrible, our travel toward light—
Unless the courage to refuse keeps doubling speed,
The courage to not avoid, excuse, or falsely hope,
Who board and clear the decks,
Word by word, deed by always dangerous deed.

Time and Speed, Appearance and all Truth,
Still in the heavens of bright peace,
Return the image as we desire.

FIVE

Six Miles Nearer Heaven

The man has spread his silver wings,
    is six miles
    nearer heaven,

has climbed the tumbleweed of cloud
    conquers where no bird
    has striven;

his wings wink joy before his breeze,
    his pockets billow
    and let loose the sky,

two streaming trails, the fountains of his play,
    lie smoking on,
    though he has catapulted by.

Am I Death?

Am I death?
Am I claimed as being its own?
Its flat walk mine

into the brightness it soon dims,
the seas it dries,
the breath whose swing it stills?

Am I become the Other Side?
Is my skin poached in the boil of the boundary line,
my hands webbed from passage through the toll?

Am I now beyond you? Faint?
Repulsive in my lack of self?
Wet and cold as—(who is this?)—with swollen lids,
                                        recede?

Have I taken death's hand?
Trudged to the precinct to which hope is never called,
where words gargle their own sweet vowels?

Most terrible, I, drowning in remembrance,
clasp backwards still, to the sun and lovely stars,
to the door where you yet stand.

I, drowning,
remember now with passionate tenderness
even those things I scorned.

I, drowning,
long only to cry out, to sing, to tap,
to say, "Before it is too late—"

I, who was star and rain, was choice of love and war,
feel no strength of flesh,
just sneaky, mortal draft, chill across an open wound.

For Mary's Last Days

as children,

running sideways when wind increased the fall of leaves,
arms flung to catch them as they fell,
vivid gold and crimsons all, and when our rakes
had heaped encircling walls
so high they hid the kitchen lights,

high enough for safety in a headlong plunge,

at last we knew a world
whose language frothed
ubiquitous as the plunge and bubble in the sea,

and just what we expected,
though not one of us could have had the mind
to conceive of its surprise,
nor could we have known the darkness,
as now leaves clung to us and left us free,
just as we knew they would
though not till that moment when we knew it.

But the taking leave,
the taking leave of life,
these precision months, days, seconds —
this act, in singularity profound,
beyond our touch,

bound in silence words can only fringe
the way the caverns of the sea
rise up and make a fringe of foam against the shore;

Nor is the touch, the fringe,
the comfort we hold forth mere comfort.
It is, rather, that the caverns are so wide
and in spite of having grown from being child,
we still have not the mind, we can't conceive,
the language and the dark to which we plunge—

    as children—

Walking the Halls of Peter Bent
Brigham Hospital Before Dawn

I

this deepest of all drift,
this quiet slack,
this candletoned aroma of dim light,

such quiet gives all quiet time.

•

the nurses sleep,
planted in deep rest,

alert
when I,
recovering from old dreams,
walk noiseless past the open doors,

fallow and lulled.

II

In the shroud of a darkened room,
a train conductor,
requiring blood beyond his own,
shifts his bones to rise from bed;

his skinny back is pale beneath his robe.

at the entrance to his room a monitor,
finger on a moving face, affirms
his beating heart, his private scrawl.

Awake, the nurse looks up.
"What's he doing?"
Before I can shape my lips to speech
she is moving softly in his room.
His old hands grope the disarray.

"I wanted to see was I still hooked up."
"Yes, you're on. You're still on. Here.
See? You look good. See? You're going good."

III

Recovering from old wounds, soft with sight,
I walk the corridors' dim light and row
through angles sewn with steel and nitrous tanks,

glimpse the loops of tube,
and legs. legs covered
with bandage. brownlegs, hairy,
legs striped with the long red scar.

More deeply gaze and see the hand at rest,
heparin locked to its own i.v.

At such depths live tubes snake the bottled air,
tankheads bubble in a slit of lidless eye,
circuitry clocks databanks of fire,

the masked face closes on oxygen.

IV

technology with humans wed tonight,

sick age
wed to the healing young;

we wed ourselves.
we sleep toward dawns,

our bodies need,
we eat and are condemned.

the nurse and the conductor walk along.

V

This deepest of all drift,
this life.
This work which we bring home.

Cover him, for he is myth,
half diving
through the scum toward night,

half risen,
bearing that for which he died.

•

Walk there then,
and keep him modest in his robe.

It's only him,
going down the distance of the globe.

Long after we have all departed

the sea,
to whom we gave its name,
will heave,
without its name,
the same.

The wind will scour the selfsame sky,
the grass cling to the selfsame rock.

As they did,
before we came.
And what I am,
will be.
without my name.

Notes

The poems in this book were written during the course of several decades. A few are from an earlier book written under the name of Elizabeth Aldrich. "Deep Shadow of the Sun" was published in 1979 in the *Partisan Review* under the title "Helios."

For many people growing up in the fifties and sixties the shadow of nuclear devastation loomed as an immediate and appalling possibility. Nor had it dissipated in 1981, when "Time Present" was written, in which I set out to make this danger seem personal and vivid. As it happened, Jonathan Schell's extraordinary series of articles in the New Yorker came out just as I was completing "Time Present." The poem is despairing in its conclusion and I include it here only because of the renewed threat of nuclear disaster—from nuclear terrorists.

I have been interested for some time in entering a poem on one voice and coming out on an entirely different voice. I call this "changing horses in midstream." "Bilious Barbara" is an example, as is "Even the Most Wounded" and "Black Wind And A Dog." Unities are fracturing and it has come to seem inadequate to truth for a poem to be so confident of its own being that it could remain the same poem throughout its course.

This is Elizabeth Elliott's second book of poetry. Elliott for many years taught the craft of poetry in the Gallatin division of New York University, where she developed New/Rhythmics, a scanning system of fourteen ideograms allowing readers to closely compare the diverse rhythms of all English language poetry and prose. Elliott co-founded and directed, for over a decade, Spectra, a performing arts organization in Columbia County using Manhattan-based musicians, dancers and actors. Elliott's ¡Cordoba!, a recreation of Moorish-ruled Spain in the tenth and eleventh centuries, was among the many productions mounted by Spectra. Elliott's first marriage was to Alexander Aldrich, with whom she had four children. She recently married the composer Clinton Elliott. They live in Tyringham, Massachusetts.